Editor
Eric Migliaccio

Managing Editor
Ina Massler Levin, M.A.

Cover Artist
Brenda DiAntonis

Art Production Manager
Kevin Barnes

Imaging
James Edward Grace

Publisher
Mary D. Smith, M.S. Ed.

FLUENCY PRACTICE

- Readers' Theater
- Ballads & Songs
- Poems
- Proverbs
- Historical Literature
- Tongue Twisters
- Fables
- Essays
- Novel Excerpts

THE CALL OF THE WILD

Author

Melissa Hart, M.F.A.

Teacher Created Resources, Inc.
6421 Industry Way
Westminster, CA 92683
www.teachercreated.com

ISBN: 978-1-4206-8042-3

©2006 Teacher Created Resources, Inc.
Reprinted, 2011
Made in U.S.A.

Table of Contents

Table of Contents *(cont.)*

Introduction

Fluency is the ability to express oneself easily and gracefully. A fluent reader demonstrates confidence with written material, based on knowledge and practice. *Fluency Practice, Grades 4 & Up* offers intermediate readers the opportunity to perfect their oral reading skills in a variety of genres, including:

- ❖ Ballads
- ❖ Poetry
- ❖ Proverbs
- ❖ Songs
- ❖ Historical Documents, Speeches, and Songs

- ❖ Tongue Twisters
- ❖ Fables
- ❖ Essays
- ❖ Monologues
- ❖ Novel Excerpts
- ❖ Readers' Theater

As children practice reading each passage aloud, pay attention to their speed. A fluent reader speaks at a comfortable pace, modulating tone periodically. Encourage children to vary their voice when reading dialog, in particular. This is particularly effective in adding interest for both readers and listeners when approaching reader's theater and short stories.

Note whether children hesitate between words. The practice of each piece in this book will ensure smooth, fluid reading at a consistent pace. Pay attention to the number of words pronounced correctly; the fluent child will read with 90–100% accuracy.

Reading aloud can be intimidating for beginners. The pieces in this book are designed to engage children in the reading process with humor, compelling plots, and exciting new words. Encourage children to read each selection several times as a group, in order to build their familiarity with vocabulary and themes. As each child begins to read aloud individually, use positive reinforcement to reward effort and fluency. After each student finishes an oral reading assignment, congratulate him or her for the accomplishment and ask the following questions:

✔ *How do you feel about the way you read the piece?*

✔ *Did you read slowly or quickly?*

✔ *Was your reading choppy or smooth?*

✔ *Did you stumble over particular words?*

✔ *How did you feel about your use of expression? Did you vary your tone?*

✔ *Did you show emotion or feeling?*

✔ *How might you read differently next time?*

Use *Fluency Practice, Grades 4 & Up* to help create enthusiastic and articulate readers!

Before You Read

A ballad is a song or poem that tells a story. The narrative ballad may be sung over centuries, undergoing changes with each new singer. Sometimes, this ballad was made into a play, most often performed in Ohio in the 1850s. The play revolves around the words to the ballad below.

The Arkansas Traveler

Oh, once upon a time in Arkansas,
An old man sat in his little cabin door
And fiddled at a tune that he liked to hear,
A jolly old tune that he played by ear.

It was raining hard but the fiddler didn't care:
He sawed away at the popular air.
Though his roof tree leaked like a waterfall,
That didn't seem to bother that man at all.

A traveler was riding by that day
And stopped to hear him a-practicing away.
The cabin was afloat, and his feet were wet,
But still the old man didn't seem to fret.

So the stranger said: "Now, the way it seems to me,
You'd better mend your roof," said he.
But the old man said as he played away:
"I couldn't mend it now, it's a rainy day."

The traveler replied: "That's all quite true,
But this, I think, is the thing for you to do:
Get busy on a day that is fair and bright,
Then pitch the old roof till it's good and tight."

But the old man kept on a-playing at his reel
And tapped the ground with his leathery heel.
"Get along," said he, "for you give me a pain.
My cabin never leaks when it doesn't rain."

~Anonymous

Before You Read

This ballad dates back to the mid-1700s. Sailors believed that the sight of a mermaid foretold of a shipwreck.

The Mermaid

'Twas Friday morn when we set sail,
And we had not got far from land,
When the Captain, he spied a lovely mermaid,
With a comb and a glass in her hand.

(Chorus)
Oh, the ocean waves may roll
And the stormy winds may blow,
While we poor sailors go skipping aloft
And the land lubbers lay down below,
below, below

And the land lubbers lay down below.
Then up spoke the Captain of our gallant ship,
And a jolly old Captain was he,
"I have a wife in Salem town,
But tonight a widow she will be."

The Mermaid *(cont.)*

(Chorus)

Then up spoke the Cook of our gallant ship,
And a greasy old Cook was he,
"I care more for my kettles and my pots
Than I do for the roaring of the sea."

(Chorus)

Then up spoke the Cabin-boy of our
gallant ship,
And a dirty little brat was he;
"I have friends in Boston town
That don't care a ha' penny for me."

(Chorus)

Then three times 'round went our
gallant ship,
And three times 'round went she,
And the third time that she went 'round
She sank to the bottom of the sea.

(Chorus)

~Anonymous

Before You Read

It is rumored that William Douglas wrote this ballad in the 1800s for his love, Annie. The tune was popular among English troops during the Crimean War. This ballad includes old Scottish words. See if you can translate them into contemporary English.

Annie Laurie

Maxwelton's braes are bonnie,
Where early fa's the dew,
And it's there that Annie Laurie
Gave me her promise true.
Gave me her promise true,
Which ne'er forgot will be,
And for bonnie Annie Laurie
I'd lay me doon and dee.

Her brow is like the snawdrift,
Her throat is like the swan,
Her face it is the fairest,
That 'er the sun shone on.
That 'er the sun shone on.
And dark blue is her e'e,
And for bonnie Annie Laurie
I'd lay me doon and dee.

Like dew on the gowan lying,
Is the fa' o' her fairy feet,
And like winds in summer sighing,
Her voice is low and sweet.
Her voice is low and sweet,
And she's a' the world to me,
And for bonnie Annie Laurie
I'd lay me doon and dee.

~Anonymous

Before You Read

Jesse James was a famous bandit in the 1800s. He went by the pseudonym "Thomas Howard." James was killed in 1892 by Robert Ford, a man he had regarded as his friend.

The Ballad of Jesse James

Jesse James was a lad that killed many a man.
He robbed the Danville train.
He stole from the rich and he gave to the poor
He'd a hand, a heart, and a brain.

It was Robert Ford, that dirty little coward
I wonder how he does feel
For he ate Jesse's bread and he slept in Jesse's bed,
And he laid Jesse James in his grave.

Jesse was a man, a friend to the poor,
He couldn't see a brother suffer pain
And with his brother Frank he robbed
the Springfield bank
And he stopped the Glendale train

It was with his brother Frank he robbed
the Gallatin Bank
And carried the money from the town
It was in this very place they had a little chase
And they shot Captain Sheets to the ground.

The Ballad of Jesse James *(cont.)*

(Chorus)

Jesse leaves a wife, that'll mourn all her life
His three children they were brave
For that dirty little coward, he shot Mr. Howard
And lay poor Jesse in his grave

It was on a Wednesday night, the moon was
shining bright
They robbed the Danville train.
The people they did say for many miles away
It was robbed by Frank and Jesse James

It was on a Friday night when the moon was
shining bright
They robbed the Glendale train
For the agent on his knees, delivered up the keys
To the outlaws Frank and Jesse James
Twas on a Saturday night and Jesse was at home
A-talking to his family so brave
Bob Ford came along like a thief in the night
And laid Jesse James in his grave.

(Chorus)

The people held their breath when they heard
of Jesse's death
And wondered how he came to die
For the big reward, Little Robert Ford
Shot Jesse James on the sly

The Ballad of Jesse James *(cont.)*

Jesse went to rest with his hand on his breast
And there are many who never saw his face
He was born one day in the county of Clay
And he came from a solitary race.

(Chorus)

Now men, when you go out into the west,
Never be afraid to die
They had the law in their hands
but they didn't have the sand
To take Jesse James alive.

This song was made by Billy Gashade
As soon as the news did arrive
He said there's no man with the law in his hand
Can take Jesse James alive

(Chorus)

A Noiseless Patient Spider

A noiseless, patient spider,
I mark'd, where, on a little promontory, it stood, isolated;
Mark'd how, to explore the vacant, vast surrounding,
It launch'd forth filament, filament, filament, out of itself;
Ever unreeling them—ever tirelessly speeding them.

And you, O my Soul, where you stand,
Surrounded, surrounded, in measureless oceans of space,
Ceaselessly musing, venturing, throwing,—seeking the spheres, to connect them;
Till the bridge you will need, be form'd—till the ductile anchor hold;
Till the gossamer thread you fling, catch somewhere, O my Soul.

~Walt Whitman

Before You Read

William Blake was an English poet who lived from 1757 to 1827. There are different versions of this poem that have different spellings for the words "watered" and "outstretched." It is thought that the original words were spelled "water'd" and "outstretch'd," or even "waterd" and "outstretchd," but the most common spelling is used below. Think about what he might be saying about friends and enemies in this poem.

A Poison Tree

I was angry with my friend:
I told my wrath, my wrath did end.
I was angry with my foe:
I told it not, my wrath did grow.

And I watered it in fears,
Night and morning with my tears:
And I sunned it with smiles
And with soft deceitful wiles.

And it grew both day and night,
Till it bore an apple bright.
And my foe beheld it shine,
And he knew that it was mine—

And into my garden stole
When the night had veiled the pole;
In the morning, glad, I see
My foe outstretched beneath the tree.

~William Blake

Before You Read

Like William Blake, William Wordsworth was also from England. He lived from 1770 to 1850 and wrote many poems about nature.

Daffodils

I WANDER'D lonely as a cloud
    That floats on high o'er vales and hills,
When all at once I saw a crowd,
    A host, of golden daffodils;
Beside the lake, beneath the trees,
Fluttering and dancing in the breeze.
Continuous as the stars that shine
    And twinkle on the Milky Way,
They stretch'd in never-ending line
    Along the margin of a bay:
Ten thousand saw I at a glance,
Tossing their heads in sprightly dance.
The waves beside them danced; but they
    Out-did the sparkling waves in glee:
A poet could not but be gay,
    In such a jocund company:
I gazed—and gazed—but little thought
What wealth the show to me had brought:
For oft, when on my couch I lie
    In vacant or in pensive mood,
They flash upon that inward eye
    Which is the bliss of solitude;
And then my heart with pleasure fills,
And dances with the daffodils.

                ~William Wordsworth

Before You Read

Emily Dickinson lived and wrote poetry in Massachusetts in the 1800s. Think about what creature she is writing about in the poem below.

A Narrow Fellow in the Grass

A narrow fellow in the grass
Occasionally rides;
You may have met him,—did you not?
His notice sudden is.

The grass divides as with a comb,
A spotted shaft is seen;
And then it closes at your feet
And opens further on.

He likes a boggy acre,
A floor too cool for corn.
Yet when a child, and barefoot,
I more than once, at morn,

Have passed, I thought, a whip-lash
Unbraiding in the sun,—
When, stooping to secure it,
It wrinkled, and was gone.

Several of nature's people
I know, and they know me;
I feel for them a transport
Of cordiality;

But never met this fellow,
Attended or alone,
Without a tighter breathing,
And zero at the bone.

~Emily Dickinson

Poetry

Before You Read

Lewis Carroll was the penname of Charles Lutwidge Dodgson. He is famous for his novel Alice in Wonderland. *Even though "Jabberwocky" is a nonsense poem, it has still managed to be translated into over 29 languages. As you read, think about what the nonsense words might mean.*

Jabberwocky

'Twas brillig, and the slithy toves
Did gyre and gimble in the wabe:
All mimsy were the borogoves,
And the mome raths outgrabe.

"Beware the Jabberwock, my son!
The jaws that bite, the claws that catch!
Beware the Jubjub bird, and shun
The frumious Bandersnatch!"

He took his vorpal sword in hand:
Long time the manxome foe he sought —
So rested he by the Tumtum tree,
And stood awhile in thought.

#8042 Fluency Practice Grades 4 & Up　　　16　　　©Teacher Created Resources, Inc.

Jabberwocky *(cont.)*

And, as in uffish thought he stood,
The Jabberwock, with eyes of flame,
Came whiffling through the tulgey wood,
And burbled as it came!

One, two! One, two! And through and through
The vorpal blade went snicker-snack!
He left it dead, and with its head
He went galumphing back.

"And, has thou slain the Jabberwock?
Come to my arms, my beamish boy!
O frabjous day! Callooh! Callay!"
He chortled in his joy.

'Twas brillig, and the slithy toves
Did gyre and gimble in the wabe;
All mimsy were the borogoves,
And the mome raths outgrabe.

~Lewis Carroll

Before You Read

Mary Howitt lived from 1799 to 1888. What advice is she giving to readers in this funny, rhyming poem?

The Spider and the Fly

"Will you walk into my parlour?" said the Spider to the Fly,
"'Tis the prettiest little parlour that ever you did spy.
The way into my parlour is up a winding stair,
And I've a many curious things to show when you are there."
Oh no, no," said the little Fly, "to ask me is in vain,
For who goes up your winding stair can ne'er come down again."

"I'm sure you must be weary, dear, with soaring up so high;
Will you rest upon my little bed?" said the Spider to the Fly.
"There are pretty curtains drawn around; the sheets are fine and thin,
And if you like to rest awhile, I'll snugly tuck you in!"
"Oh no, no," said the little Fly, "for I've often heard it said,
They never, never wake again, who sleep upon your bed!"

Said the cunning Spider to the Fly, " Dear friend what can I do
To prove the warm affection I've always felt for you?
I have within my pantry good store of all that's nice;
I'm sure you're very welcome — will you please to take a slice?"
"Oh no, no," said the little Fly, "kind Sir, that cannot be,
I've heard what's in your pantry, and I do not wish to see!"

"Sweet creature!" said the Spider, "you're witty and you're wise,
How handsome are your gauzy wings, how brilliant are your eyes!
I've a little looking-glass upon my parlour shelf,
If you'll step in one moment, dear, you shall behold yourself."
"I thank you, gentle sir," she said, "for what you're pleased to say,
And bidding you good morning now, I'll call another day."

The Spider and the Fly *(cont.)*

The Spider turned him round about, and went into his den,
For well he knew the silly Fly would soon come back again:
So he wove a subtle web, in a little corner sly,
And set his table ready, to dine upon the Fly.

Then he came out to his door again, and merrily did sing,
"Come hither, hither, pretty Fly, with the pearl and silver wing;
Your robes are green and purple — there's a crest upon your head;
Your eyes are like the diamond bright, but mine are dull as lead!"

Alas, alas! how very soon this silly little Fly,
Hearing his wily, flattering words, came slowly flitting by;
With buzzing wings she hung aloft, then near and nearer drew,
Thinking only of her brilliant eyes, and green and purple hue —

Thinking only of her crested head — poor foolish thing!
At last, Up jumped the cunning Spider, and fiercely held her fast.
He dragged her up his winding stair, into his dismal den,
Within his little parlour — but she ne'er came out again!

And now dear little children, who may this story read,
To idle, silly flattering words, I pray you ne'er give heed:
Unto an evil counsellor, close heart and ear and eye,
And take a lesson from this tale, of the Spider and the Fly.

~Mary Howitt

Before You Read

A proverb is a short statement of truth. How many of the following proverbs hold true in your life?

A book is like a garden carried in the pocket.

~Arab proverb

A clear conscience is a soft pillow.

~German proverb

A penny saved is a penny gained.

~Scottish proverb

It is not a secret if it is known by three people.

~Irish proverb

He who would climb the ladder must begin at the bottom.

~English proverb

20

Before You Read
Many proverbs are about animals.

When the mouse laughs at the cat, there is a hole nearby.

~Nigerian proverb

An old rat is a brave rat.

~French proverb

Don't look a gift horse in the mouth.

~proverb of unknown origin

Every dog hath its day.

~English proverb

If you are great, even your dog will wear a proud look.

~Japanese proverb

Before You Read

Notice while you are reading the proverbs in this book that many of the themes are universal. For example, all of the following proverbs are about patience and understanding—even though they come from different countries all over the world.

It takes time to build castles. Rome was not built in a day.

~Irish proverb

Keep a green tree in your heart and perhaps a singing bird will come.

~Chinese proverb

As we live, so we learn.

~Yiddish proverb

Clouds gather before a storm.

~proverb of unknown origin

Deal with the faults of others as gently as with your own.

~Chinese proverb

Before You Read

The following are inspirational proverbs, often used to give people hope, aspiration, and confidence.

Today is the first day of the rest of your life.

~North-American saying

There is no strength without unity.

~Irish proverb

The world is a rose: smell it and pass it on to your friends.

~Persian proverb

Better to light a candle than to curse the darkness.

~Chinese proverb

When there is no enemy within, the enemies outside cannot hurt you.

~African proverb

Before You Read

A song is a piece of writing set to music. Katherine Lee Bates lived from 1859 to 1929. She was both a poet and an English professor. Bates wrote "America the Beautiful" after being inspired by the view from Pike's Peak in Colorado.

America the Beautiful

O beautiful for spacious skies,
For amber waves of grain,
For purple mountain majesties
Above the fruited plain!

America! America!
God shed His grace on thee,
And crown thy good
With brotherhood,
From sea to shining sea!
O beautiful for pilgrim feet
Whose stern impassion'd stress
A thoroughfare for freedom beat
Across the wilderness.

America! America!
God mend thine ev'ry flaw,
Confirm thy soul
In self-control,
Thy liberty in law.

America the Beautiful *(cont.)*

O beautiful for heroes prov'd
In liberating strife,
Who more than self their country loved,
And mercy more than life.

America! America!
May God thy gold refine
Till all success
Be nobleness,
And ev'ry gain divine.

O beautiful for patriot dream
That sees beyond the years
Thine alabaster cities gleam
Undimmed by human tears.

America! America!
God shed His grace on thee,
And crown thy good
With brotherhood
From sea to shining sea.

~Katherine Lee Bates

Before You Read

This song was written by Barker Bradford around 1885. Many parodies have been done to this tune, including a Halloween favorite called "Oh, My Darling Frankenstein."

Clementine

In a cavern, in a canyon
Excavating for a mine
Lived a miner forty-niner
And his daughter, Clementine.

Oh, my darling, oh, my darling
Oh, my darling Clementine
You are lost and gone forever
Dreadful sorry, Clementine.

Light she was and like a fairy
And her shoes were number nine
Herring boxes without topses
Sandals were for Clementine.
Drove her ducklings to the water
Every morning just at nine.
Hit her foot against a splinter
Fell into the foaming brine.

Oh, my darling, oh, my darling
Oh, my darling Clementine.
You are lost and gone forever
Dreadful sorry, Clementine.

Clementine *(cont.)*

Ruby lips above the water
Blowing bubbles soft and fine
But alas, I was no swimmer

So I lost my Clementine.
Then the miner, forty-niner
Soon began to peak and pine
Thought he oughta join his daughter

Now he's with his Clementine.
Oh, my darling, oh, my darling
Oh, my darling Clementine
You are lost and gone forever
Dreadful sorry, Clementine

There's a churchyard on the hillside
Where the flowers grow and twine
There grow roses, 'mongst the posies
Fertilized by Clementine

Oh, my darling, oh, my darling
Oh, my darling Clementine
You are lost and gone forever
Dreadful sorry, Clementine.

~Barker Bradford

Before You Read

No one is sure who wrote the words and music to this song, but it may have originated among slaves in the southern United States. It was introduced as a written piece of music in the 1840s by Daniel Decatur Emmett.

Polly Wolly Doodle

Oh, I went down South
For to see my Sal
Sing Polly wolly doodle all the day.
My Sal, she is
A spunky gal
Sing Polly wolly doodle all the day.

(Chorus)

Fare thee well,
Fare thee well,
Fare thee well my fairy fay
For I'm going to Lou'siana
For to see my Susyanna
Sing Polly wolly doodle all the day.

Oh, my Sal, she is
A maiden fair
Sing Polly wolly doodle all the day.
With curly eyes
And laughing hair
Sing Polly wolly doodle all the day.

(Chorus)

Behind the barn,
Down on my knees
Sing Polly wolly doodle all the day.

Polly Wolly Doodle *(cont.)*

I thought I heard
A chicken sneeze
Sing Polly wolly doodle all the day.

(Chorus)

He sneezed so hard
With the whooping cough
Sing Polly wolly doodle all the day.

He sneezed his head
And the tail right off
Sing Polly wolly doodle all the day.

(Chorus)

Oh, a grasshopper sittin'
On a railroad track
Sing Polly wolly doodle all the day.

A-pickin' his teeth
With a carpet tack
Sing Polly wolly doodle all the day.

(Chorus)

Oh, I went to bed
But it wasn't any use
Sing Polly wolly doodle all the day
My feet stuck out
Like a chicken roost
Sing Polly wolly doodle all the day.

(Chorus)

~Anonymous

Songs

Before You Read

The lyrics of this song are attributed to Harry "Haywire Mac" McClintock, who lived in Knoxville, Tennessee. The song is from the perspective of a type of man called a "hobo," someone who didn't hold a steady job but rather traveled by railroad looking for handouts. An often seen subtitle to the song is "Hobo's Paradise."

The Big Rock Candy Mountains

In the Big Rock Candy Mountains
There's a land that's fair and bright
Where the handouts grow on bushes
And you sleep out ev'ry night
Where the boxcars are all empty
And the sun shines ev'ry day
Oh, I'm bound to go where there ain't no snow
Where the rain don't fall and the wind don't blow
In the Big Rock Candy Mountains.

In the Big Rock Candy Mountains
You never change your socks
And little streams of lemonade
Come a-tricklin' down the rocks
The hobos there are friendly
And their fires all burn bright
There's a lake of stew and soda, too
You can paddle all around 'em in a big canoe
In the Big Rock Candy Mountains.

~Harry McClintock

Before You Read

This is an old favorite, an American cowboy song. Though many believe it originated in Texas, it actually started among British troops who came to Manitoba in the late 1860s. Another version has been found that was sung by the early fur traders.

Red River Valley

From this valley they say you are going
We will miss your bright eyes and sweet smile
For they say you are taking the sunshine

That has brightened our path for a while.
Come and sit by my side if you love me
Do not hasten to bid me adieu
But remember the Red River Valley
And the girl who has loved you so true.

Won't you think of the valley you're leaving
Oh, how lonely, how sad it will be?
Oh, think of the fond heart you're breaking
And the grief you are causing to me.

Come and sit by my side if you love me
Do not hasten to bid me adieu
But remember the Red River Valley
And the girl who has loved you so true.

I have promised you, darling, that never
Will a word from my lips cause you pain;
And my life, it will be yours forever
If you only will love me again.

Come and sit by my side if you love me
Do not hasten to bid me adieu
But remember the Red River Valley
And the girl who has loved you so true.

~Anonymous

Before You Read

"Señor Don Gato" is a traditional song from Mexico. It is about a cat who is so excited to be getting married that he sings of his love up into the open sky—and falls off the roof.

Señor Don Gato

Oh, Señor Don Gato was a cat.
On a high red roof Don Gato sat.
He went there to read a letter,
Meow, meow, meow,
Where the reading light was better,
Meow, meow, meow.

'Twas a love note for Don Gato.
"I adore you," wrote the lady cat
Who was fluffy, white, and nice, and fat.
There was not a sweeter kitty,
Meow, meow, meow,
In the country or the city,
Meow, meow, meow,
And she said she'd wed Don Gato.

Oh, Don Gato jumped so happily
He fell off the roof and broke his knee.
Broke his ribs and all his whiskers,
Meow, meow, meow.
And his little solar plexus,
Meow, meow, meow,
"¡Ay Caramba!" cried Don Gato.

32

Señor Don Gato *(cont.)*

Then the doctors all came on the run
Just to see if something could be done,
And they held a consultation,

Meow, meow, meow,
About how to save their patient,
Meow, meow, meow.
How to save Señor Don Gato.
But in spite of everything they tried,
Poor Señor Don Gato up and died,
And it wasn't very merry,
Meow, meow, meow,
Going to the cemetery,
Meow, meow, meow,
For the ending of Don Gato.

When the funeral passed the market square
Such a smell of fish was in the air.
Though his burial was slated,

Meow, meow, meow,
He became reanimated,
Meow, meow, meow.
He came back to life, Don Gato

~Anonymous

Before You Read

This is Australia's national song. Even though it may seem like it is filled with nonsense words (like "Jabberwocky"), the words are actually real terms, most of which are still used in Australia. The song is about a man who steals a sheep and gets caught by the police.

Waltzing Matilda

Once a jolly swagman
Camped by a billabong,
Under the shade
Of a coolibah tree,
And he sang as he watched
And waited 'til his billy boiled:
"You'll come a-waltzing,
Matilda, with me.
Waltzing Matilda,
Waltzing Matilda
You'll come a-waltzing,
Matilda, with me."
And he sang as he watched
And waited 'til his billy boiled:
"You'll come a-waltzing,
Matilda, with me."
Down came a jumbuck
To drink at the billabong,
Up jumped the swagman
And grabbed him with glee,
And he sang as he stowed
That jumbuck in his tucker bag:
"You'll come a-waltzing,
Matilda, with me.
Waltzing Matilda,
Waltzing Matilda,
You'll come a-waltzing,
Matilda, with me."

Waltzing Matilda *(cont.)*

"Where's that jolly jumbuck
You've got in your tucker bag?
And he sang as he stowed
That jumbuck in his tucker bag,
"You'll come a-waltzing,
Matilda, with me."
Down rode the squatter,
Mounted on his thoroughbred,

Up came the troopers,
One, two, three,
"You'll come a-waltzing,
Matilda, with me."
Waltzing Matilda,
Waltzing Matilda,
You'll come a-waltzing,
Matilda, with me.
Where's that jolly jumbuck
You've got in your tucker bag?
You'll come a-waltzing,
Matilda, with me."
Up jumped the swagman,
Sprang into the billabong,
"You'll never catch me
Alive," said he,
And his ghost may be heard
As you pass by the billabong:
"You'll come a-waltzing,
Matilda, with me.
Waltzing Matilda,
Waltzing Matilda,
You'll come a-waltzing,
Matilda, with me."
And his ghost may be heard
As you pass by the billabong:
"You'll come a-waltzing,
Matilda, with me."

~Andrew Barton "Banjo" Patterson

Before You Read

The national anthem of the United States was written by Francis Scott Key on September 20, 1814. A lawyer and poet, Key witnessed the bombing of Fort Henry in Maryland and then wrote "The Star Spangled Banner." It was adopted at the United States' national anthem in 1931.

The Star Spangled Banner

Oh, say can you see, by the dawn's early light
What so proudly we hailed at the twilight's last gleaming?
Whose broad stripes and bright stars, through the perilous fight,
O'er the ramparts we watched, were so gallantly streaming?
And the rockets' red glare, the bombs bursting in air
Gave proof through the night that our flag was still there.
O say, does that star-spangled banner yet wave
O'er the land of the free and the home of the brave?

On the shore, dimly seen through the mists of the deep,
Where the foe's haughty host in dread silence reposes,
What is that which the breeze o'er the towering steep,
As it fitfully blows now conceals, now discloses?
Now it catches the gleam of the morning's first beam,
In full glory reflected now shines on the stream:
'Tis the star-spangled banner! O, long may it wave
O'er the land of the free and the home of the brave.

And where is that band who so vauntingly swore
That the havoc of war and the battle's confusion
A home and a country should leave us no more?
Their blood has wiped out their foul footsteps' pollution;
No refuge could save the hireling and slave
From the terror of flight or the gloom of the grave:
And the star-spangled banner in triumph doth wave
O'er the land of the free and the home of the brave.

Oh! thus be it ever, when freemen shall stand
Between their loved homes and the war's desolation!
Blest with victory and peace, may the heaven-rescued land
Praise the Power that hath made and preserved us a nation.
Then conquer we must, for our cause, it is just;
And this be our motto: "In God is our trust."
And the star-spangled banner forever shall wave
O'er the land of the free and the home of the brave!

~Francis Scott Key

Before You Read

The United States Constitution was completed on September 17, 1787, and adopted by the original thirteen states in the U.S. The Preamble outlines the goals of the seven original Articles of the Constitution.

Preamble to the Constitution of the United States

We the People of the United States, in Order to form a more perfect Union, establish Justice, insure domestic Tranquility, provide for the common defence, promote the general Welfare, and secure the Blessings of Liberty to ourselves and our Posterity, do ordain and establish this Constitution for the United States of America.

Before You Read

The Bill of Rights refers to the first ten amendments of the United States Constitution, adopted in 1789. It was written soon after the adoption of the Constitution in order to limit the power of the federal government.

The Bill of Rights

First Amendment

Congress shall make no law respecting an establishment of religion, or prohibiting the free exercise thereof; or abridging the freedom of speech, or of the press; or the right of the people peaceably to assemble, and to petition the Government for a redress of grievances.

Second Amendment

A well regulated Militia, being necessary to the security of a free State, the right of the people to keep and bear Arms shall not be infringed.

Third Amendment

No Soldier shall, in time of peace be quartered in any house, without the consent of the Owner, nor in time of war, but in a manner to be prescribed by law.

Fourth Amendment

The right of the people to be secure in their persons, houses, papers, and effects, against unreasonable searches and seizures, shall not be violated, and no Warrants shall issue, but upon probable cause, supported by Oath or affirmation, and particularly describing the place to be searched, and the persons or things to be seized.

Fifth Amendment

No person shall be held to answer for a capital, or otherwise infamous crime, unless on a presentment or indictment of a Grand Jury, except in cases arising in the land or naval forces, or in the Militia, when in actual service in time of War or public danger; nor shall any person be subject for the same offence to be twice put in jeopardy of life or limb; nor shall be compelled in any criminal case to be a witness against himself, nor be deprived of life, liberty, or property, without due process of law; nor shall private property be taken for public use, without just compensation.

The Bill of Rights *(cont.)*

Sixth Amendment

In all criminal prosecutions, the accused shall enjoy the right to a speedy and public trial, by an impartial jury of the State and district wherein the crime shall have been committed, which district shall have been previously ascertained by law, and to be informed of the nature and cause of the accusation; to be confronted with the witnesses against him; to have compulsory process for obtaining witnesses in his favor, and to have the Assistance of Counsel for his defence.

Seventh Amendment

In suits at common law, where the value in controversy shall exceed twenty dollars, the right of trial by jury shall be preserved, and no fact tried by a jury, shall be otherwise reexamined in any Court of the United States, than according to the rules of the common law.

Eighth Amendment

Excessive bail shall not be required, nor excessive fines imposed, nor cruel and unusual punishments inflicted.

Ninth Amendment

The enumeration in the Constitution, of certain rights, shall not be construed to deny or disparage others retained by the people.

Tenth Amendment

The powers not delegated to the United States by the Constituiton, nor prohibited by it to the states, are reserved to the states respectively, or to the people.

Before You Read

British military officers first sang Yankee Doodle to make fun of the "Yankees" with whom they served during the French and Indian War. The term "doodle" meant a fool. During the Revolutionary War, United States soldiers adopted the song and made it their own.

Yankee Doodle

Father and I went down to camp,
Along with Captain Gooding;
And there we saw the men and boys,
As thick as hasty pudding.

Yankee doodle, keep it up,
Yankee doodle dandy;
Mind the music and the step,
And with the girls be handy.

There was Captain Washington
Upon a slapping stallion,
A-giving orders to his men,
I guess there was a million.

And then the feathers on his hat,
They looked so' tarnal fin-a,
I wanted pockily to get
To give to my Jemima.

And then we saw a swamping gun,
Large as a log of maple;
Upon a deuced little cart,
A load for father's cattle.

And every time they shoot it off,
It takes a horn of powder;
It makes a noise like father's gun,
Only a nation louder.

I went as nigh to one myself,
As Siah's underpinning;
And father went as nigh agin,
I thought the deuce was in him.

Yankee Doodle *(cont.)*

We saw a little barrel, too,
The heads were made of leather;
They knocked upon it with little clubs,
And called the folks together.

And there they'd fife away like fun,
And play on cornstalk fiddles,
And some had ribbons red as blood,
All bound around their middles.

The troopers, too, would gallop up
And fire right in our faces;
It scared me almost to death
To see them run such races.

Uncle Sam came there to change
Some pancakes and some onions,
For 'lasses cake to carry home
To give his wife and young ones.

But I can't tell half I see
They kept up such a smother;
So I took my hat off, made a bow,
And scampered home to mother.

Cousin Simon grew so bold,
I thought he would have cocked it;
It scared me so I streaked it off,
And hung by father's pocket.

And there I saw a pumpkin shell,
As big as mother's basin;
And every time they touched it off,
They scampered like the nation.

Yankee doodle, keep it up,
Yankee doodle dandy;
Mind the music and the step,
And with the girls be handy.

Before You Read

Ralph Waldo Emerson wrote "The Concord Hymn" for the dedication of a battle monument commemorating the contributions of Concord citizens during the first battle of the American Revolution. It was sung at the completion of the monument, called the Obelisk, on July 4, 1837.

The Concord Hymn

By the rude bridge that arched the flood,
Their flag to April's breeze unfurled,
Here once the embattled farmers stood,
And fired the shot heard round the world.

The foe long since in silence slept;
Alike the conqueror silent sleeps;
And Time the ruined bridge has swept
Down the dark stream which seaward creeps.

On this green bank, by this soft stream,
We set to~day a votive stone;
That memory may their deed redeem,
When, like our sires, our sons are gone.

Spirit, that made those heroes dare
To die, or leave their childern free,
Bid Time and Nature gently spare
The shaft we raise to them and thee.

~Ralph Waldo Emerson

Before You Read

Abraham Lincoln delivered this address on November 19, 1863, during the American Civil War. Although it took only a few minutes to read, The Gettysburg Address is regarded as one of the greatest speeches in history.

The Gettysburg Address

Fourscore and seven years ago our fathers brought forth on this continent a new nation, conceived in liberty, and dedicated to the proposition that all men are created equal.

Now we are engaged in a great civil war, testing whether that nation, or any nation so conceived and so dedicated, can long endure. We are met on a great battle-field of that war. We have come to dedicate a portion of that field as a final resting-place for those who here gave their lives that this nation might live. It is altogether fitting and proper that we should do this.

But, in a larger sense, we cannot dedicate . . . we cannot consecrate . . . we cannot hallow . . . this ground. The brave men, living and dead, who struggled here, have consecrated it far above our poor power to add or detract. The world will little note nor long remember what we say here, but it can never forget what they did here. It is for us, the living, rather, to be dedicated here to the unfinished work which they who have fought here have thus far so nobly advanced. It is rather for us to be here dedicated to the great task remaining before us . . . that from these honored dead we take increased devotion to that cause for which they here gave the last full measure of devotion; that we here highly resolve that these dead shall not have died in vain; that this nation, under God, shall have a new birth of freedom; and that government of the people, by the people, for the people, shall not perish from the earth.

~Abraham Lincoln

Before You Read

A tongue twister depends on repetition of a particular sound that "twists" your tongue when you try to say it aloud. This type of repetition is called alliteration. See if you can say the tongue twisters below.

A cricket critic licked
a crinkled ticket.

A proper cup of coffee from
a copper coffee pot.

Eight gray geese grew
greedy over gravy.

The big book crook took
the big cookbook.

Before You Read

Can you make your own tongue twister? Use the examples below for ideas.

Shirley sheared six soiled sheep
in the shiny sheep shed.

Baby Boy Blue blew big
bright bubbles.

Six sharp, shifty sharks
squashed a school of shrimp.

A black bug bit a big black bear.
But where is the big black bear
that the big black bug bit?

Before You Read

This tongue twister is also a type of poem called a limerick. All limericks have five lines, two that rhyme with each other, and another three that rhyme with each other. Listen to the cadence of the poem as you read it out loud.

A certain young fellow named Beebee

Wished to marry a lady named Phoebe.

"But," he said, "I must see

What the minister's fee be

Before Phoebe be Phoebe Beebee!"

Before You Read

This tongue twister brings up the fact that a woodchuck is an animal that has no ability to "chuck" (toss, throw) wood. How do you think the author came up with the idea for this poem?

How much wood
would a woodchuck chuck
if a woodchuck could chuck wood?
He would chuck, he would, as much
as he could,
And chuck as much as a
woodchuck would
If a woodchuck could chuck wood.

*Tongue Twisters*

Before You Read

This tongue twister makes use of the words "toed" and "toad." These two words are homophones, words that sound the same but have different meanings.

A tree-toad loved a she-toad
Who lived up in a tree.
He was a two-toed tree-toad,
But a three-toed toad was she.
The two-toed tree-toad tried to win
The three-toed she-toad's heart,
For the two-toed tree-toad
loved the ground
That the three-toed tree-toad trod.
But the two-toed tree-toad
tried in vain;
He couldn't please her whim.
From her tree-toad bower,
With her three-toed power,
The she-toad vetoed him.

#8042 Fluency Practice Grades 4 & Up   48   ©Teacher Created Resources, Inc.

Before You Read

This tongue twister also uses homonyms, as well as words that, when combined, make a new, compound word (seesaw).

Mr. See owned a saw.
And Mr. Soar owned a seesaw.
Now, See's saw sawed Soar's seesaw
Before Soar saw See,
Which made Soar sore.
Had Soar seen See's saw
Before See sawed Soar's seesaw,
See's saw would not have sawed
Soar's seesaw.
So, See's saw sawed Soar's seesaw.
But it was sad to see Soar so sore
just because See's saw sawed
Soar's seesaw.

Before You Read

It takes 21 pounds of cow's milk to make one pound of butter. There are records of butter's use as early 2000 B.C.

Betty Botter had some butter,
"But," she said, "this butter's bitter.
If I bake this bitter butter,
It would make my batter bitter.
But a bit of better butter,
That would make my batter better."

So she bought a bit of butter —
Better than her bitter butter —
And she baked it in her batter;
And the batter was not bitter.
So 'twas better Betty Botter
Bought a bit of better butter.

Before You Read

The term "sour grapes," which means to deny your desire for something because you can't get it, was derived from this fable.

The Fox and the Grapes

One hot summer's day, Fox was walking through an orchard when he came to a bunch of grapes ripe and purple on a vine. "Just the thing to quench my thirst," he said.

Fox took a run and a jump but missed the bunch. He turned around again and cried, "One, two, three!" He jumped up but missed the grapes again. Once more, Fox tried to reach the tempting grapes. At last, he gave up and walked away with his nose in the air, saying: "I am sure those grapes are sour."

Moral: It is easy to scorn what you cannot get.

~Aesop

Before You Read

A fable is a short story that offers a moral lesson. Aesop was an ancient Greek writer who narrated dozens of fables that were handed down from generation to generation as part of the oral tradition.

The Ant and the Dove

An ant marched to the bank of a river to quench its thirst and fell into the stream. It was just about to drown, when a dove, who sat in a tree overhanging the water, saw the ant's predicament and plucked a leaf, letting it fall into the stream close to her.

The ant climbed onto the leaf and floated in safety to the bank. "Oh, thank you," the ant cried to the dove.

Shortly afterwards, a bird catcher tromped down toward the river. He stood under the tree, and laid a trap for the dove, who sat in the branches preening her feathers.

The ant, understanding what the man was about to do, stung him in the foot. In pain, the bird catcher threw down the trap, causing a terrible racket.

The dove flew off, escaping harm.

Moral: One good turn deserves another

~Aesop

Before You Read

The following fable is about two men who encounter a bear and their two very different reactions to the situation. How do you think you would react if that happened to you?

The Bear and the Two Travelers

Two men were traveling together, when a bear met them on their path. "Grrrr!" it cried.

One of the men quickly climbed up into a tree and concealed himself in the branches. The other man, seeing that he was about to be attacked, fell flat on the ground.

The bear lumbered up, felt him with his snout, and smelt him all over. Then he snuffled something in his ear.

The man held his breath and pretended the appearance of death as much as he could. The bear soon left him, for it is said that bears will not touch a dead body.

When the bear had walked away, the other man descended from the tree. Laughing, he asked his friend what it was the bear had whispered in his ear.

"He gave me this advice," his fellow traveler replied. "Never travel with a friend who deserts you at the approach of danger."

Moral: Misfortune tests the sincerity of friends.

~Aesop

Before You Read

This fable is about a crow that invents an ingenious way of getting water out of a pitcher. Did you know that many inventions were actually mistakes? Post-It notes stemmed from a failed super glue experiment, and Popsicles came to be when a boy, after stirring his cup of fruit-flavored soda with a stick, left it out in the cold overnight and came back to find it frozen with the stirring stick standing straight up in it!

The Crow and the Pitcher

A crow nearly dying of thirst spotted a pitcher down below her on the ground. Hoping to find it filled with water, she flew to it with delight.

When she reached the pitcher, she discovered sadly that it contained just a little water at the very bottom. She tried everything she could think of to reach the water, but all her efforts were in vain.

"I must get creative," the crow said at last. She collected as many pebbles as she could carry in her beak and dropped them one by one into the pitcher. Slowly, the water level rose, until finally the crow could drink from the pitcher. Thus, she saved her own life.

Moral: Necessity is the mother of invention.

~Aesop

Before You Read

In this fable, a father ties a bundle of sticks together to show how hard it is to break them when they are all together. Sailors made rope for boats in a similar way. Rope is composed of many strands of twine or string that, when braided together, is much stronger than the original material itself.

The Father and His Sons

A father had a family of sons who were always quarreling among themselves. He decided to show them the problem with arguing.

"Bring me a bundle of sticks," he commanded.

When they had brought him a thick bundle of sticks from an elm tree, he placed the bundle into the hands of each of them. "Now, break this bundle into pieces," he said.

Each brother tried with all his strength, but they were not able to break the bundle.

The father opened the bundle and divided the sticks among the brothers. "Now, break them into pieces," he commanded. Now each brother broke his few sticks easily.

Then, the father said, "My sons, if you unite to assist each other, you will be as this bundle, strong in spite of all the attempts of your enemies to break you. However, if you are divided among yourselves, you will be broken as easily as these sticks."

Moral: United we stand; divided we fall.

~Aesop

Before You Read

Many stories are similar to the fable below about a mouse helping a lion. One of the themes in this fable, (a small creature being able to do something a larger creature can't), is repeated in many stories. For example, The Little Engine That Could *is a story about a small train that went up a track that the bigger engines couldn't.*

The Lion and the Mouse

A lion was awakened from sleep by a mouse running over his furry face. The lion rose up in fury and grabbed the mouse in his large paws. He was just about to eat the tiny creature when the mouse threw up his little paws and begged, "If only you'll spare my life, I will repay your kindness."

"Ha ha ha! How could a little mouse like you help me?" The lion laughed and let the mouse go.

Shortly after this incident, hunters captured the lion and wrapped strong ropes around his body. The lion roared in pain.

The mouse, recognizing the lion's roar, ran toward him. Quickly, he gnawed the rope with his teeth and set the lion free. "You laughed at the idea of my being able to help you," said the mouse, "but now you know that it is possible for even a little mouse to help a great lion!"

Moral: Little friends may prove to be great friends.

~Aesop

Before You Read

After reading the fable below, decide whether you think this is a fair contest or not. If not, what contest would you have to see which is stronger?

The Wind and the Sun

The Wind and the Sun had an argument about which was the stronger being. "I'm stronger because I can blow the leaves off the trees," cried the Wind.

"I'm stronger because my heat allows the trees to give birth to the leaves," answered the Sun.

Suddenly they saw a traveler walking down the road. The Sun said: "I know how we may settle our dispute. Whichever of us can cause that man to remove his cloak shall be regarded as the stronger being. Agreed?"

"Agreed," said the Wind.

So the Sun disappeared behind a large gray cloud, and the Wind began to blow as hard as it could upon the traveler. It puffed out its cheeks and made a ferocious roaring sound. But the harder the Wind blew, the more tightly did the traveler wrap his cloak around his body. At last, the Wind had to give up in despair.

Then the Sun came out and shone warm and golden upon the traveler. The man soon found it too hot to walk with his cloak on, and he removed it.

"Ah ha!" cried the Sun. "I gave this traveler warmth and light, and so I am the stronger being."

The Wind bowed its head in agreement.

Moral: Kindness is more effective than severity.

~Aesop

Before You Read

If you were a mouse in this fable, what suggestion would you give to outwit the cat. If you like the "belling the cat" idea, how would you go about getting the bell on the cat?

Belling the Cat

Long ago, the mice elected a general council to consider what they might do to outwit their common enemy, the Cat.

Some mice suggested a trick, and other mice suggested a trap. At last, a young mouse stood up. "I have a proposal," he told the assembled mice. "You will all agree," said he, "that our chief danger lies in the sly and silent manner in which the Cat approaches us. If we could hear some signal of her approach, we could easily escape from her!"

All the mice around him began to prick up their ears. "Keep talking!" they cried.

The young mouse continued. "I propose, therefore, that we procure a small bell and attach it by a ribbon around the Cat's neck. Then, we will always know when she is about, and we could easily escape while she is roaming our neighborhood."

All of the mice applauded wildly and cheered for the young mouse. Then, an older mouse stood and held up one paw for silence. "That is all very well," he said, "but who is brave enough to bell the Cat?"

The mice looked at one another. For a long moment, nobody spoke. The young mouse shuffled his feet and cleared his throat, embarrassed. And then the older and wiser mouse delivered this moral: "It is easy to suggest impossible solutions."

~Aesop

Before You Read

An essay is a piece of writing that explains and makes observations on a particular topic. The following essay is about great-horned owls. There are over 200 species of owls.

Great-Horned Owls

Great-horned owls are often called the "tigers of the forest." They get this name because they can live almost anywhere and eat almost anything. Also, they only have one predator.

Great-horned owls make their nests in old, abandoned stick nests made by other birds. They also nest at the edge of cliffs, and in the hollows of trees. They live in forested rural areas, but can also survive happily in neighborhoods which have tall trees.

These owls, which weigh between three and five pounds, can lift prey larger than themselves! They eat rodents, snakes, frogs, smaller birds, and even skunks. Tiny grooves on their flight feathers allow wind to pass over them silently so that they can surprise their prey. They catch it with their strong talons and rip it into pieces with their sharp beaks.

Great-horned owls have only one predator: humans. Sometimes, the owls get electrocuted on fencing or wire. They also get hit by cars. Sometimes, their territory may be destroyed if someone cuts down a forest.

Rehabilitation centers across the world work hard to protect these fascinating birds. Some evening, you may hear a soft hooting and feel the wind from silent wings pass over your face. Then you'll know that you have been visited by one of these "tigers of the forest."

The Art of Photography

Photography is an art form that has existed for well over a century. With even an inexpensive camera, beginning photographers can create memorable and beautiful images that can be used in a variety of ways.

There are many different types of cameras. You may choose to use a digital camera that transfers images to a computer. You may decide that you want a camera that uses print film, which you must take to be developed. Alternatively, you might want to learn to develop the film yourself. Whatever type of camera you use, there are a few things to remember before you take a picture.

First, compose your picture carefully. Look at the background around your subject and make sure that there is nothing distracting in the frame. Also, pay attention to the head and feet of your subject. Be sure that these are also in the frame.

You can use several techniques to make your photos beautiful. The ideal time to photograph is in the early morning and evening, when the light is softest. When photographing people, you should position them so that the sun is behind them. Otherwise, they may be squinting into the light.

Once you have developed a nicely-composed photograph, you may choose to do many things with it. First, you might create a photo album. Some photographers create an album on their own webpage. Photographs can be transferred to calendars, mugs, T-shirts, and other items for a wonderful gift. Finally, you could put your finished photo in a frame on your dresser to remind you of your accomplishments in photography!

Before You Read

In the last paragraph of this essay about backpacking, the author writes about being a smart camper and keeping food away from bears. Did you know that bears are attracted to anything with an odor? This includes soap, sunscreen, deodorant, toothpaste, and garbage.

The Joy of Backpacking

Backpacking is a sport that allows you to get plenty of exercise while spending time in the wilderness and learning valuable survival skills. You, too, can backpack—just remember to pack smart and be prepared for all types of weather.

Potential backpackers need just a few crucial items. First, you need a backpack big enough to hold a rolled-up sleeping bag, a sleeping pad, a camp stove, matches, and a cooking pot. Don't forget a spoon! Take lightweight food like oats and ramen—foods that can be easily prepared with water. It is critical to take a water filter so that you don't get an upset stomach from bacteria in a river or stream.

On a backpacking adventure, you might experience sun, rain, wind, and even snow. Dress in three layers of waterproof clothing, and don't forget a hat. You'll want a pair of dry socks for sleeping. In cooler weather, mittens are also important. Good backpackers always bring a tarp—this comes in handy as a lean-to if you get stuck in a rainstorm.

Backpacking allows you to observe nature up close. There's nothing like the feeling of eating pizza you've made over your single-burner stove under a full moon. But make sure you're a smart camper. Cross streams and rivers with extreme caution, and be aware of potential hazards on the trail. At night, stow your food high in a tree, away from wild animals. Otherwise, you might find yourself sharing your sleeping bag with a bear!

Before You Read

The essay below describes the pleasures and responsibilities of keeping a rabbit as a pet. There are over 50 different species of rabbit, the most recently discovered one being a striped rabbit found in the mountains of Laos and Vietnam.

Rabbits Make Good Pets

Have you ever wondered what it would be like to own a rabbit as a pet? Rabbits are wonderful, loving animals that can be trained to use a litter box, and even to play ball!

First, consider allowing your rabbit to live in the house. House rabbits learn easily to use a litter box so that they don't ruin your carpet and furniture. Make sure to give them plenty of chew toys so that they don't gnaw on your table legs. It is also important to hang electrical cords up high so that your rabbit doesn't try to eat them for a snack.

Rabbits need a little care each day. Brush your pet, and make sure toenails are trimmed short to prevent scratching. Most rabbits love to be scratched behind the ears and on the head. Using a reward such as carrot or apple pieces, you can train your rabbit to come to you when you call it. It will get to know and love you.

Rabbits enjoy playing with a variety of toys. They love to crawl inside and on top of boxes. They enjoy throwing small, lightweight plastic toys up into the air. Rabbits also like balls. You can roll a ball to your rabbit and train it to nudge the ball back to you.

The best part about having a rabbit is the affection that you receive from your pet. A rabbit will sit on your lap and allow you to pet it. It will even nuzzle your face and hair. Although your rabbit can't purr like a cat or bark like a dog, if you listen closely, it will tell you how much it loves you.

Before You Read

The essay below describes how to train for a 5K race. The fastest 5K time on record is held by an Ethiopian man who ran it in 13:23 —13 minutes and 23 seconds.

You Can Run a 5K Race!

Have you ever wondered what it would feel like to race through a finish line, heart pounding, as the crowd around you cheers? Running a 5K race isn't difficult, as long as you prepare for it beforehand and observe a few important details on race day.

First, make a running schedule. You should train for about three months before your first race. Start by jogging just one lap around your local track or for ten minutes on a field or sidewalk. Make sure to allow a few minutes afterwards to cool down and stretch. Every week, add a little more distance, a little more time, until eventually you can run an entire 5K, or 3.1 miles.

You don't need much equipment to be a runner—just a good pair of running shoes. Make sure that they have plenty of support and that they fit well. Different people run in different ways, depending on the construction of your foot. A good shoe salesperson will study your footprint and your running stride and choose a shoe that's right for you.

When race day arrives, eat a light meal two hours before your starting time. Oatmeal, bananas, or bagels are popular choices among runners. Warm up before the race by jogging for ten minutes. As the race begins, start out slow and steady so that you have plenty of energy to finish. Make sure to enjoy the race as you run it, taking time to look around at the scenery. And don't forget to pat yourself on the back as you burst across the finish line. You deserve it!

Before You Read

The essay below describes writing to an author. Many authors now have their own websites. You can find titles of other books they have written, background about them, and even writing tips.

Write to an Author

Have you ever read a book from cover to cover, then wished you could contact the author? Children's authors love to receive mail from their readers. They want to know which books you've enjoyed. Sometimes, they even write back!

As you begin to write your letter to your favorite author, think about what you liked most about his or her book. Describe your favorite scene or character. Don't forget to tell the author a little about yourself, as well. Include your name, age, city or town, and perhaps a few hobbies. You may want to write a rough draft of your letter and then copy it onto nice paper.

Authors don't always list their address in the phone book or on the Internet. The best way to contact your favorite author is to send a letter care of his or her publisher. You can find the publisher's address near the front of the book. On your envelope, write your author's name and then "care of" below it. Then, copy down the publisher's name and address. Don't forget a stamp!

If you have included your return address, you might open your mailbox one day to find a surprise! Sometimes, an author is busy working on a new book and doesn't have time to write back just then, so you might receive a form letter instead of a personal one. But sometimes, you may receive a letter written by your favorite author just to you!

Before You Read

In the 1800s, many pioneer families moved west in the hopes of buying land. With so many people moving to the United States (specifically, to the East Coast) from Europe, crowding became an issue for quite a few. Other families moved in order to look for better, higher-paying jobs. Still others were moving to be closer to family who were already out west and raving about it.

Laura Ingalls Wilder

Laura Ingalls Wilder is the famous author of the *Little House on the Prairie* series. Although she didn't know it at the time, her childhood experiences as part of an early American pioneer family would entertain millions of children and adults all over the world for decades.

Laura was born in 1867 in Wisconsin. Her family moved several times during her childhood and endured many hardships. Grasshoppers destroyed their crops, and blizzards threatened food supplies. Laura's baby brother died, and her sister lost her eyesight at age 15. These are only some of the events which Laura wrote about in her books.

She also wrote about many happy memories. Fiddle music and oranges and trips to the general store in town were exciting to a little girl who lived in a log cabin and, later, a sod house. Laura's vivid descriptions in the pages of her books help readers to picture what it was like to live in her century.

Laura's books continue to be successful because she so carefully recorded the sights, sounds, smells, and tastes of her childhood. If she were alive today, she might advise young writers to keep a daily journal to record their own day-to-day life.

Laura was 65 when her first book, *Little House in the Big Woods*, was published. She wrote 18 books in all before she died at age 90 in Missouri. Her books inspired the television series *Little House on the Prairie*, which first aired in 1974. If you love Laura Ingalls Wilder's books, you might also love the TV program. Perhaps both will inspire you to write your own book!

Before You Read

A monologue is a speech given by one character. This monologue is delivered by Alice after she spots the White Rabbit running away from her. She chases after him and falls down a hole.

Alice in Wonderland

ALICE: Why, how impolite of him. I asked him a civil question, and he pretended not to hear me. That's not at all nice.

I say, Mr. White Rabbit, where are you going? Hmmm. He won't answer me. And I do so want to know what he is late for. I wonder if I might follow him. Why not? There's no rule that I mayn't go where I please. I . . . I will follow him. Wait for me, Mr. White Rabbit. I'm coming, too!

(Alice falls.)

How curious. I never realized that rabbit holes were so dark . . . And so long . . . And so empty. I believe I have been falling for five minutes, and I still can't see the bottom! Hmph! After such a fall as this, I shall think nothing of tumbling downstairs. How brave they'll all think me at home. Why, I wouldn't say anything about it even if I fell off the top of the house! I wonder how many miles I've fallen by this time.

I must be getting somewhere near the center of the earth. I wonder if I shall fall right through the earth! How funny that would be. Oh, I think I see the bottom. Yes, I'm sure I see the bottom. I shall hit the bottom, hit it very hard, and oh, how it will hurt!

~Lewis Carroll

Before You Read

Huckleberry Finn delivers this monologue about being frustrated when he doesn't get what he has prayed for. Notice the words below that are written in vernacular—that is, speech particular to a people in a certain place or time. In this case, the place and time is Mississippi during the 1800s.

The Adventures of Huckleberry Finn

HUCK: Miss Watson told me to pray every day, and whatever I asked for I would get it. But it warn't so. I tried it. Once I got a fish-line, but no hooks. It warn't any good to me without hooks. I tried for the hooks three or four times, but somehow I couldn't make it work. By and by, one day, I asked Miss Watson to try for me, but she said I was a fool. She never told me why, and I couldn't make it out no way. I set down one time back in the woods, and had a long think about it. I says to myself, if a body can get anything they pray for, why don't Deacon Winn get back the money he lost on pork? Why can't the widow get back her silver snuffbox that was stole? Why can't Miss Watson fat up? No, says I to my self, there ain't nothing in it. I went and told the widow about it, and she said the thing a body could get by praying for it was "spiritual gifts." This was too many for me, but she told me what she meant—I must help other people, and do everything I could for other people, and look out for them all the time, and never think about myself. This was including Miss Watson, as I took it. I went out in the woods and turned it over in my mind a long time, but I couldn't see no advantage about it— except for the other people; so at last I reckoned I wouldn't worry about it any more, but just let it go.

~Mark Twain

Before You Read

This monologue is spoken by Juliet, a young women in love with a young man named Romeo in Shakespeare's famous play. Shakespeare wrote this play in the late 1500s. Notice how his language differs from the language we use today.

Romeo and Juliet

JULIET: Thou knowest the mask of night is on my face;
Else would a maiden blush bepaint my cheek
For that which thou hast heard me speak to-night.
Fain would I dwell on form — fain, fain deny
What I have spoke; but farewell compliment!
Dost thou love me? I know thou wilt say 'Ay';
And I will take thy word. Yet, if thou swear'st,
Thou mayst prove false. At lovers' perjuries,
They say Jove laughs. O gentle Romeo,
If thou dost love, pronounce it faithfully.
Or if thou thinkest I am too quickly won,
I'll frown, and be perverse, and say thee nay,
So thou wilt woo; but else, not for the world.
In truth, fair Montague, I am too fond,
And therefore thou mayst think my 'havior light;
But trust me, gentleman, I'll prove more true
Than those that have more cunning to be strange.
I should have been more strange, I must confess,
But that thou overheard'st, ere I was ware,
My true-love passion. Therefore pardon me,
And not impute this yielding to light love,
Which the dark night hath so discovered.

~William Shakespeare

Before You Read

Shakespeare wrote this play in the late 1500s. In this monologue, the character Jacques discusses the seven stages of life.

As You Like It

All the world's a stage,
And all the men and women merely players:
They have their exits and their entrances;
And one man in his time plays many parts,
His acts being seven ages. At first the infant,
Mewling and puking in the nurse's arms.
And then the whining school-boy, with his satchel
And shining morning face, creeping like snail
Unwillingly to school. And then the lover,
Sighing like furnace, with a woeful ballad
Made to his mistress' eyebrow. Then a soldier,
Full of strange oaths and bearded like the pard,
Jealous in honour, sudden and quick in quarrel,
Seeking the bubble reputation
Even in the cannon's mouth. And then the justice,
In fair round belly with good capon lined,
With eyes severe and beard of formal cut,
Full of wise saws and modern instances;
And so he plays his part. The sixth age shifts
Into the lean and slipper'd pantaloon,
With spectacles on nose and pouch on side,
His youthful hose, well saved, a world too wide
For his shrunk shank; and his big manly voice,
Turning again toward childish treble, pipes
And whistles in his sound. Last scene of all,
That ends this strange eventful history,
Is second childishness and mere oblivion,
Sans teeth, sans eyes, sans taste, sans everything.

~William Shakespeare

Before You Read

Smirnov is the proprietor of a country estate in this famous one-act play. In this comic monologue, he complains about love and women.

The Boor

SMIRNOV: I don't understand how to behave in the company of ladies. Madam, in the course of my life I have seen more women than you have sparrows. Three times have I fought duels for women, twelve I jilted and nine jilted me. There was a time when I played the fool, used honeyed language, bowed and scraped. I loved, suffered, sighed to the moon, melted in love's torments. I loved passionately, I loved to madness, loved in every key, chattered like a magpie on emancipation, sacrificed half my fortune in the tender passion, until now the devil knows I've had enough of it. Your obedient servant will let you lead him around by the nose no more. Enough! Black eyes, passionate eyes, coral lips, dimples in cheeks, moonlight whispers, soft, modest sights— for all that, madam, I wouldn't pay a kopeck! I am not speaking of present company, but of women in general; from the tiniest to the greatest, they are conceited, hypocritical, chattering, odious, deceitful from top to toe; vain, petty, cruel with a maddening logic and in this respect, please excuse my frankness, but one sparrow is worth ten of the aforementioned petticoat-philosophers. When one sees one of the romantic creatures before him he imagines he is looking at some holy being, so wonderful that its one breath could dissolve him in a sea of a thousand charms and delights; but if one looks into the soul—it's nothing but a common crocodile.

~Anton Chekhov

Before You Read

Oscar Wilde wrote this comic play about social manners in the late 1800s. Mabel Chiltern gives this monologue, in which she complains about her boyfriend Tommy for how he proposes marriage.

An Ideal Husband

MABEL CHILTERN: Well, Tommy has proposed to me again. Tommy really does nothing but propose to me. He proposed to me last night in the music-room, when I was quite unprotected, as there was an elaborate trio going on. I didn't dare to make the smallest repartee, I need hardly tell you. If I had, it would have stopped the music at once. Musical people are so absurdly unreasonable. They always want one to be perfectly dumb at the very moment when one is longing to be absolutely deaf. Then he proposed to me in broad daylight this morning, in front of that dreadful statue of Achilles. Really, the things that go on in front of that work of art are quite appalling. The police should interfere. At luncheon I saw by the glare in his eye that he was going to propose again, and I just managed to check him in time by assuring him that I was a bimetallist. Fortunately I don't know what bimetallism means. And I don't believe anybody else does either. But the observation crushed Tommy for ten minutes. He looked quite shocked. And then Tommy is so annoying in the way he proposes. If he proposed at the top of his voice, I should not mind so much. That might produce some effect on the public. But he does it in a horrid confidential way. When Tommy wants to be romantic he talks to one just like a doctor. I am very fond of Tommy, but his methods of proposing are quite out of date. I wish, Gertrude, you would speak to him, and tell him that once a week is quite often enough to propose to any one, and that it should always be done in a manner that attracts some attention.

~Oscar Wilde

Before You Read

A novel is a fiction story, generally longer than 100 pages. Here is a page from Louisa May Alcott's classic 19th-century novel Little Women. *You might want to assign different people to read the voices of sisters Meg, Jo, Beth, and Amy.*

"A Merry Christmas"

Jo was the first to wake in the grey dawn of Christmas morning. No stockings hung at the fireplace, and for a moment she felt as much disappointed as she did long ago, when a little sock fell down because it was so crammed with goodies. Then she remembered her mother's promise, and, slipping her hand under her pillow, drew out a little crimson-covered book. She knew it very well, for it was that beautiful story of the best life ever lived, and Jo felt that it was a true guide-book for any pilgrim going the long journey. She woke Meg with a "Merry Christmas," and bade her see what was under her pillow. A green-covered book appeared with the same picture inside, and a few words written by their mother, which made their one present very precious in their eyes. Presently Beth and Amy woke, to rummage and find their little books also — one, dove-coloured, the other blue; and all sat looking at and talking about them, while the east grew rosy with the coming day.

In spite of her small vanities, Margaret had a sweet a pious nature, which unconsciously influenced her sisters especially Jo, who loved her very tenderly, and obeyed her because her advice was so gently given.

"A Merry Christmas" *(cont.)*

"Girls," said Meg seriously, looking from the tumbled head beside her to the two little night-capped ones in the room beyond, "Mother wants us to read and love and mind these books, and we must begin at once. We used to be faithful about it; but since Father went away, and all this war trouble unsettled us, we have neglected many things. You can do as you please; but I shall keep my book on the table here, and read a little every morning as soon as I wake for I know it will do me good, and help me through the day."

Then she opened her new book and began to read. Jo put her arm round her, and, leaning cheek to cheek, read also with the quiet expression so seldom seen on her restless face.

"How good Meg is! Come, Amy, let's do as they do. I'll help you with the hard words, and they'll explain things if we don't understand," whispered Beth, very much impressed by the pretty books and her sisters' example. "I'm glad mine is blue," said Amy; and then the rooms were very still while the pages were softly turned, and the winter sunshine crept in to touch the bright heads and serious faces with a Christmas greeting.

~Louisa May Alcott

Before You Read

Black Beauty *is the story of a horse that travels far and has many adventures—some happy and some harmful—before finding a home with a loving owner.*

"My Early Home"

The first place that I can well remember was a large pleasant meadow with a pond of clear water in it. Some shady trees leaned over it, and rushes and water-lilies grew at the deep end. Over the hedge on one side we looked into a plowed field, and on the other we looked over a gate at our master's house, which stood by the roadside; at the top of the meadow was a grove of fir trees, and at the bottom a running brook overhung by a steep bank.

While I was young I lived upon my mother's milk, as I could not eat grass. In the daytime I ran by her side, and at night I lay down close by her. When it was hot we used to stand by the pond in the shade of the trees, and when it was cold we had a nice warm shed near the grove. As soon as I was old enough to eat grass my mother used to go out to work in the daytime, and come back in the evening.

There were six young colts in the meadow besides me; they were older than I was; some were nearly as large as grown-up horses. I used to run with them, and had great fun; we used to gallop all together round and round the field as hard as we could go. Sometimes we had rather rough play, for they would frequently bite and kick as well as gallop.

One day, when there was a good deal of kicking, my mother whinnied to me to come to her, and then she said:

"My Early Home" *(cont.)*

"I wish you to pay attention to what I am going to say to you. The colts who live here are very good colts, but they are cart-horse colts, and of course they have not learned manners. You have been well-bred and well-born; your father has a great name in these parts, and your grandfather won the cup two years at the Newmarket races; your grandmother had the sweetest temper of any horse I ever knew, and I think you have never seen me kick or bite. I hope you will grow up gentle and good, and never learn bad ways; do your work with a good will, lift your feet up well when you trot, and never bite or kick even in play."

I have never forgotten my mother's advice; I knew she was a wise old horse, and our master thought a great deal of her. Her name was Duchess, but he often called her Pet.

Our master was a good, kind man. He gave us good food, good lodging, and kind words; he spoke as kindly to us as he did to his little children. We were all fond of him, and my mother loved him very much. When she saw him at the gate she would neigh with joy, and trot up to him. He would pat and stroke her and say, "Well, old Pet, and how is your little Darkie?" I was a dull black, so he called me Darkie; then he would give me a piece of bread, which was very good, and sometimes he brought a carrot for my mother. All the horses would come to him, but I think we were his favorites. My mother always took him to the town on a market day in a light gig.

~Anna Sewell

Before You Read

The Call of the Wild is a book about a dog stolen from his home. Buck, the dog, is treated cruelly and made to work hard as a sled dog before returning to his freedom in the wilderness.

"Into the Primitive"

Buck lived at a big house in the sun-kissed Santa Clara Valley. Judge Miller's place, it was called. It stood back from the road, half hidden among the trees, through which glimpses could be caught of the wide cool veranda than ran around its four sides. The house was approached by gravelled driveways which wound about through wide-spreading lawns and under the interlacing boughs of tall poplars. At the rear things were on even a more spacious scale than at the front. There were on great stables, a where a dozen grooms and boys held forth, rows of vine-clad servants' cottages, an endless and orderly array of outhouses, long grape arbors, green pastures, orchards, and berry patches. Then there was the pumping plant for the artesian well, and the big cement tank where Judge Miller's boys took their morning plunge and kept cool in the hot afternoon.

And over this great demense Buck ruled. Here he was born, and here he had lived the four years of his life. It was true, there were other dogs. There could not but be other dogs on so vast a place, but they did not count. They came and went, resided in the populous kennels, or lived obscurely in the recesses of the house after the fashion of Toots, the Japanese pug, or Ysabel, the Mexican hairless—strange creatures that rarely put nose out of doors or set foot to ground. On the other hand, there were the fox terriers, a score of them at least, who yelped fearful promises at Toots and Ysabel looking out of the windows at them and protected by a legion of housemaids armed with brooms and mops.

"Into the Primitive" *(cont.)*

But Buck was neither house-dog nor kennel dog. The whole realm was his. He plunged into the swimming tank or went hunting with the Judge's sons; he escorted Mollie and Alice, the Judge's daughters, on long twilight or early morning rambles; on wintry nights he lay at the Judge's feet before the roaring library fire; he carried the Judge's grandsons on his back, or rolled them in the grass, and guarded their footsteps through wild adventures down to the fountain in the stable yard, and even beyond, where the paddocks were, and the berry patches. Among the terriers he stalked imperiously, and Toots and Ysabel he utterly ignored, for he was king—king over all creeping, crawling, flying things of Judge Miller's place, humans included.

His father, Elmo, a huge St. Bernard, had been the Judge's inseparable companion, and Buck bid fair to follow in the way of his father. He was not so large—he weighed only one hundred and forty pounds—for his mother, Shep, had been a Scotch shepherd dog. Nevertheless, one hundred and forty pounds, to which was added the dignity that comes of good living and universal respect, enabled him to carry himself in right royal fashion. During the four years since his puppy-hood he had lived the life of a sated aristocrat; he had a fine pride in himself, was ever a trifle egotistical, as country gentlemen sometimes become because of their insular situation. But he had saved himself by not becoming a mere pampered house-dog. Hunting and kindred outdoor delights had kept down the fat and hardened his muscles; and to him, as to the cold-tubbing races, the love of water had been a tonic and a health preserver.

~Jack London

> **Before You Read**
> The Jungle Book *was published in 1894. It tells the story of Mowgli, a boy raised by wolves in the jungles of India. Before you read the following excerpt, choose one person to read the part of Father Wolf, another to read the part of Tabaqui, and a third person to read the part of Mother Wolf.*

"Mowgli's Brothers"

It was seven o'clock of a very warm evening in the Seeonee hills when Father Wolf woke up from his day's rest, scratched himself, yawned, and spread out his paws one after the other to get rid of the sleepy feeling in their tips. Mother Wolf lay with her big grey nose dropped across her four tumbling, squealing cubs, and the moon shone into the mouth of the cave where they all lived. "Augrh!" said Father Wolf, "it is time to hunt again," and he was going to spring downhill when a little shadow with a bushy tail crossed the threshold and whined: "Good luck go with you, O Chief of the Wolves; and good luck and strong white teeth go with the noble children, that they may never forget the hungry in this world."

It was the jackal—Tabaqui, the Dish-licker—and the wolves of India despise Tabaqui because he runs about making mischief, and telling tales, and eating rags and pieces of leather from the village rubbish-heaps. But they are afraid of him too, because Tabaqui, more than anyone else in the Jungle—ever afraid of anyone, and runs through the forest biting everything in his way. Even the tiger runs and hides when little Tabaqui goes mad, for madness is the most disgraceful thing that can overtake a wild creature. We call it hydrophobia, but they call it *dewanee*—the madness—and run.

"Enter, then, and look," said Father Wolf stiffly; "but there is no food here."

"For a wolf, no," said Tabaqui; "but for so mean a person as myself a dry bone is a good feast. Who are we, the *Gidur-log* (the Jackal-People), to pick and choose?"

"Mowgli's Brothers" *(cont.)*

He scuttled to the back of the cave, where he found the bone of a buck with some meat on it, and sat cracking the end merrily.

"All thanks for this good meal," he said, licking his lips. "How beautiful are the noble children! How large are their eyes! And so young too! Indeed, indeed, I might have remembered that the children of kings are men from the beginning."

Now, Tabaqui knew as well as anyone else that there is nothing so unlucky as to compliment children to their faces, and it pleased him to see Mother and Father Wolf look uncomfortable.

Tabaqui sat still, rejoicing in the mischief that he had made, then he said spitefully, "Shere Khan, the Big One, has shifted his hunting-grounds. He will hunt among these hills for the next moon, so he has told me."

Shere Khan was the tiger who lived near the Waingunga River, twenty miles away.

"He has no right!" Father Wolf began angrily. "By the Law of the Jungle he has no right to change his quarters without due warning. He will frighten every head of game within ten miles, and I—I have to kill for two, these days."

"His mother did not call him Lungri (the Lame one) for nothing," said Mother Wolf quietly. "He has been lame in one foot from his birth. That is why he has only killed cattle. Now the villagers of the Waingunga are angry with him, and he has come here to make our villagers angry. They will scour the Jungle for him when he is far away, and we and our children must run when the grass is set alight. Indeed, we are very grateful to Shere Khan!"

"Shall I tell him of your gratitude?" said Tabaqui.

"Out!" snapped Father Wolf. "Out and hunt with thy master. Thou hast done harm enough for one night."

"I go," said Tabaqui quietly. "Ye can hear Shere Khan below in the thickets. I might have saved myself the message."

~Rudyard Kipling

Before You Read

This excerpt from Peter Pan *describes the Mermaids' Lagoon in Neverland. As you read this beautiful description, think about how Wendy feels about the lagoon.*

"The Mermaids' Lagoon"

If you shut your eyes and are a lucky one, you may see at times a shapeless pool of lovely pale colours suspended in the darkness; then if you squeeze your eyes tighter, the pool begins to take shape, and the colours become so vivid that with another squeeze they must go on fire. But just before they go on fire you see the lagoon. This is the nearest you ever get to it on the mainland, just one heavenly moment; if there could be two moments you might see the surf and hear the mermaids singing.

The children often spent long summer days on this lagoon, swimming or floating most of the time, playing the mermaid games in the water, and so forth. You must not think from this that the mermaids were on friendly terms with them; on the contrary, it was among Wendy's lasting regrets that all the time she was on the island she never had a civil word from one of them. When she stole softly to the edge of the lagoon she might see them by the score, especially on Marooners' Rock, where they loved to bask, combing out their hair in a lazy way that quite irritated her; or she might even swim, on tiptoe as it were, to within a yard of them, but then they saw her and dived, probably splashing her with their tails, not by accident, but intentionally.

They treated all the boys in the same way, except of course Peter, who chatted with them on Marooners' Rock by the hour, and sat on their tails when they got cheeky. He gave Wendy one of their combs.

"The Mermaids' Lagoon" *(cont.)*

The most haunting time at which to see them is at the turn of the moon, when they utter strange wailing cries; but the lagoon is dangerous for mortals then, and until the evening of which we have now to tell, Wendy had never seen the lagoon by moonlight, less from fear, for of course Peter would have accompanied her, than because she had strict rules about every one being in bed by seven. She was often at the lagoon, however, on sunny days after rain, when the mermaids come up in extraordinary numbers to play with their bubbles. The bubbles of many colours made in rainbow water they treat as balls, hitting them gaily from one to another with their tails, and trying to keep them in the rainbow till they burst. The goals are at each end of the rainbow, and the keepers only are allowed to use their hands. Sometimes hundreds of mermaids will be playing in the lagoon at a time, and it is quite a pretty sight.

But the moment the children tried to join in they had to play by themselves, for the mermaids immediately disappeared. Nevertheless we have proof that they secretly watched the interlopers, and were not above taking an idea from them; for John introduced a new way of hitting the bubble, with the head instead of the hand, and the mermaid goal-keepers adopted it. This is the one mark that John has left on the Neverland.

It must also have been rather pretty to see the children resting on a rock for half an hour after their midday meal. Wendy insisted on their doing this, and it had to be a real rest even though the meal was make-believe. So they lay there in the sun, and their bodies glistened in it, while she sat beside them and looked important.

~J.M Barrie

Before You Read

Recycling aluminum cans saves 95% of the energy needed to make aluminum from bauxite ore. In one year, recycling aluminum can save enough electricity to light a large city for six years.

Reduce, Reuse, Recycle!

Characters

- Narrator
- Tomás
- Anna
- Sandy
- Pat

Narrator:	We are in a classroom full of first-grade students. Four older students are giving a presentation.
Tomás:	Today, we'd like to talk with you about recycling and how it can help to reduce waste on the earth. Recycling doesn't have to be difficult.
Anna:	It takes hardly any time at all. Once you get in the habit of recycling, it's actually fun!
Sandy:	Recycling can be an extremely creative process.
Pat:	And you can even make money!
Narrator:	The older students hold up posters on which they've drawn illustrations of their topics.
Tomás:	The average American generates approximately five pounds of garbage a day. By recycling, we can reduce landfills and pollution.
Anna:	My family has three bins in our utility room—one for paper, one for plastic, and one for aluminum. Once a day, we put newspapers, yogurt containers, and cans in the bins instead of just tossing them in the trash.

82

Reduce, Reuse, Recycle! *(cont.)*

Sandy: My mother makes wrapping paper out of grocery bags and pencil holders out of recycled orange juice cans.

Pat: My father saves bottles and cans, and then we go to the local supermarket to cash them in for money!

Narrator: The older children put away their posters. The younger children watch as they each put on a funny costume.

Tomás: I'm an old tennis shoe. You may be tempted to throw me into the trash, but people make me into athletic tracks for people's communities.

Anna: I'm a plastic soda bottle. Don't throw me in a landfill. I can be recycled to create warm and beautiful blankets.

Sandy: I'm a brown paper grocery bag. You can cut a potato in half and carve a design into it, then dip it in poster paint and decorate me all over. Presto—I'm ready to wrap up a present!

Pat: I'm an empty oatmeal container. Cover me with colored paper and buttons or sequins. Cut a small slit in my top, and I'm a bank, just waiting for your spare change.

Narrator: The first~grade students applaud. The older students bow.

Tomás, Anna, Sandy, and Pat: Thank you for listening. And remember, REDUCE, REUSE, and RECYCLE!

Declaring Our Independence

Characters

- Narrator
- Thomas Jefferson
- Benjamin Franklin
- John Adams
- Abigail Adams
- George Washington

Narrator: The year is 1776. The place is the thirteen original colonies of the United States of America. Thomas Jefferson runs up to Benjamin Franklin's porch and pounds on his door.

Jefferson: Ben! Wake up! Have you read this pamphlet by Thomas Paine?

Franklin: Tom, it's four o' clock in the morning. What pamphlet?

Jefferson: It's called "Common Sense." Paine writes that true freedom lies in total independence from England.

Franklin: Tom, that's common sense. How do you expect to win such freedom?

Jefferson: We've got to write a document that will explain exactly what we want—that is, that the political connection between ourselves and England be dissolved.

Narrator: Benjamin Franklin nods and pulls on a coat over his pajamas.

Franklin: Let's go wake up John Adams.

Narrator: Thomas Jefferson and Benjamin Franklin run up to John Adams' porch and pound on his door.

John Adams: Men, it's four thirty in the morning. Can't this wait?

Declaring Our Independence *(cont.)*

Jefferson and Franklin: No!

Narrator: Later, all three men sit hunched over a table, writing and rewriting. They cross out words and add new ones. Finally, the document is finished. They send a copy to George Washington, who is fighting in the Revolutionary War.

Washington: Fellow soldiers, I have here a marvelous piece of writing that I would like to read you. It will remind you of why we are fighting the British. It will boost your spirits and give you hope.

Narrator: John Adams writes a letter to his wife. She receives it and reads it to her friends.

Abigail Adams: "The second day of July, 1776, will begin the most memorable epoch in the history of America. . . . It ought to be solemnized with pomp and parade, with shows, games, sports, guns, bells, bonfires, and illuminations, from one end of this continent to the other, from this time forward for evermore." Why, the second of July sounds like a wonderful party!

Narrator: But although Congress voted secretly in favor of independence from Britain on July 2nd, the actual Declaration of Independence was adopted by Congress on July 4th, 1776.

Jefferson: Thank you, gentlemen, for seeing the power and strength of this document.

Franklin: With this declaration, we will gain freedom at last.

John Adams: Next year, we will celebrate the first anniversary of the Declaration of Independence with parades and fireworks and . . .

Jefferson, Franklin, and John Adams: And liberty and justice for all!

Before You Read

Imagine you have a friend, relative, or neighbor who is sick. What would you do to help them feel better? What types of things could you do for them that they can't do for themselves when they are sick?

Helping Mrs. Lee

Characters

- Narrator
- Eva
- Sam
- Phil
- Marcus
- Mrs. Lee

Narrator:	Eva, Sam, and Phil are best friends. Every day, they pass an elderly woman down the street on their way to school. Sometimes, Mrs. Lee is out pruning her roses. Other times, she's walking her dog. But one week, she doesn't appear at all.
Eva:	I wonder where Mrs. Lee has been.
Sam:	Maybe she's on vacation.
Phil:	Maybe she moved away.
Marcus:	Look! There's her dog in the window.
Narrator:	All four children look at the poodle, who peers out of the window and barks.
Eva:	Maybe we shouldn't bother her.
Sam:	I'm afraid of her.
Phil:	But what if she's hurt?
Marcus:	I'm going to go knock on her door!
Narrator:	They all run up to the doorstep and knock politely. In a minute, Mrs. Lee comes to the door in her robe and slippers.
Marcus:	Excuse me, Mrs. Lee. We were just wondering if you're feeling all right. We didn't see you in the yard.
Mrs. Lee:	I had to go into the hospital for an operation. The doctor told me to stay in bed for two weeks. Thank you for checking up on me. It's so hard to be sick.
Eva:	We'd better get to school!
Narrator:	The children go to school. The next day, they walk past Mrs. Lee's house, thinking hard.

Helping Mrs. Lee *(cont.)*

Sam:	I wish we could help her.
Phil:	But what can we do? We're just kids.
Eva:	Her dog is in the window again.
Narrator:	Again, the children look at the poodle. Then, Marcus smiles.
Marcus:	I have an idea. Meet me in front of Mrs. Lee's house after school.
Eva, Sam, and Phil:	We'll be there.
Narrator:	At three o'clock, the children gather in front of Mrs. Lee's house. Marcus hands out pieces of paper.
Marcus:	We may just be kids, but there are lots of things we can do to help Mrs. Lee.
Narrator:	The other children look at their pieces of paper.
Eva:	I'll prune her rosebushes.
Sam:	I'll walk her dog.
Phil:	I'll mow her lawn.
Narrator:	Marcus waves his piece of paper in the air.
Marcus:	And I'll bring in her newspaper and ask if she'd like me to read to her.
Narrator:	The children run up to Mrs. Lee's door and knock. She opens the door.
Mrs. Lee:	What can I do for you, children?
Eva:	We're here to see what we can do for you. I'm here to prune your rosebushes.
Sam:	I'm here to walk your dog.
Phil:	I'm here to mow your lawn.
Narrator:	Marcus holds out the newspaper.
Marcus:	I'm here to read to you . . . that is, if you'd like me to.
Narrator:	Mrs. Lee's eyes fill with tears.
Mrs. Lee:	Oh, this is wonderful. Marcus, I would love it if you'd read to me.
Narrator:	Then she gives all the children a big smile.
Mrs. Lee:	And as soon as I'm better, I'll make you all a big batch of my famous chocolate-coconut-walnut cookies!

A Trip to the Raptor Center

Characters

- Mr. Evans, a teacher
- Maria, director of the Raptor Care Center
- Jon, a student
- Kit, a student
- Colin, a student

Mr. Evans: Welcome to the Raptor Care Center, class. Today, we will learn all about raptors. I'd like to introduce Maria, the director of the center.

Maria: It's a pleasure to meet all of you. Can anyone tell me what a raptor is?

Jon (raising hand): It's a bird, right?

Maria: Yes, it's a bird of prey. The word raptor means "to seize." Raptors grasp prey in their talons and use their strong beak to rip food apart.

Kit: What kinds of birds are raptors?

Maria: That's a wonderful question! Raptors include hawks, eagles, owls, falcolns, osprey, and kites.

Colin: Why do they need a raptor care center?

Maria: That's another excellent question. Raptors can sustain illness and injuries, just like any other creature. I maintain this care center to help nurse them back to health after they get sick or injured.

Mr. Evans: Think about this, class. What types of injuries might a raptor get?

Jon: One time my mom and I were fishing, and we saw a hawk trapped in fishing line that someone had left on the ground. We cut it free, but we think it hurt its leg.

A Trip to the Raptor Center *(cont.)*

Maria: It sounds like you may have saved that hawk's life. It's important to pick up and throw away any fishing line you see, even if it's not yours.

Kit: Sometimes, a bird flies into our window. Does that ever happen to raptors?

Maria: Not usually. More often, a raptor such as a screech owl will get hit by a car. If the driver hears a thud, he or she should get out of the car and try to find out what was hit. Sometimes, we can set broken wings or legs on raptors and nurse them back to health.

Colin: My grandfather was plowing up his field and ran over a nest of burrowing owls. They all escaped, but he felt really bad.

Maria: Burrowing owls often lose their nests because of plowing or development. I'm caring for a young burrowing owl right now who lost one eye when she got hit with a haying machine.

Mr. Evans: That's horrible. Will she survive?

Maria: Yes, I think so. Sometimes, people accidentally cause harm to raptors, but we can also help them. Does anyone remember how?

Jon: We can throw away fishing line so hawks don't get tangled in it.

Kit: We can drive our cars slowly and carefully and stop to help injured wildlife.

Colin: My grandfather should walk all over his field before he plows, just in case a burrowing owl is living there.

Maria: It sounds like you all learned a lot about raptor care today.

Mr. Evans: Thanks to you, Maria.

Maria: It's my pleasure. And now, who wants to have lunch with a real live great-horned owl?

**Jon,
Kit, and
Colin:** I do!

Maria: The owl eats mice. Hopefully, you brought sandwiches.

Mr. Evans: They did. And here in my bag, I have . . . owl~shaped cookies!

**Jon,
Kit, and
Colin:** Yay!

A Short History of the United States

Characters

- Narrator
- Sherman
- Sarah

- John
- Frank
- Cynthia

- Richard
- Sumaya

Narrator: Today, we will present a short history of the United States. The U.S. has a long and fascinating history. Here are a few of the highlights.

Sherman: For centuries, Native Americans hunted and fished on this land. They moved with the seasons, gathering food according to location and weather. My great-great-grandparents were Cherokee Indians.

Sarah: My ancestors came to this country from England in the 1600s. They were Puritans, in search of religious freedom. When they arrived on the east coast, they found Native Americans willing to offer them food and assistance. Life was difficult at first; harsh winters and illness took their toll on the Puritans. But my family survived with help.

John: The leaders of the thirteen original colonies that made up the United States grew frustrated with British rule. The King of England demanded that colonists pay taxes to his government. A group of men decided that they must ask for freedom. They wrote the Declaration of Independence in 1776. This was a document which helped Americans to gain their very own government.

A Short History of the United States *(cont.)*

Frank: In the 1800s and 1900s, waves of immigrants from all parts of the world rushed to the United States. My ancestors came from Ireland. They came to Ellis Island on a ship and lived in a tiny apartment until they found jobs in a factory. They had to work very long hours, but eventually they could afford their own house.

Cynthia: My family comes from Mexico. Originally, California was part of Mexico. In the 1840s, it became part of the United States. My ancestors have lived on this land for hundreds of years.

My great-grandmother makes tamales from a recipe handed down from her great-grandmother. I'm proud to be able to speak both Spanish and English in our country.

Richard: In the 1970s and 1980s, many immigrants arrived from the Phillipines and Vietnam. I came to the United States as a child with my parents and sister. We were happy to find a nice place to live. My parents own a store, and my sister and I help them on the weekends. At home, we eat my mother's authentic Filipino food. At school, I like the cafeteria's pizza!

Sumaya: My family came to the United States from the Middle East last year. We are Muslim, and we appreciate the freedom we have to practice our religion here. I love to play rugby and soccer. I hope to become a foreign ambassador someday.

Narrator: The United States has been called a melting pot of all nationalities. The people before you today, with their various histories and experiences, are all very different, and yet they all share great joy at living in this country that has been home to so many people for so long.

Before You Read

This script is an abbreviated account of the discussions at the Constitutional Convention relating to the nature of the presidency, which the Founding Fathers were creating. There are seven speaking parts.

Constitutional Convention

Characters

- Narrator
- Elbridge Gerry
- Benjamin Franklin
- Edmund Randolph
- Alexander Hamilton
- John Dickinson
- James Madison

Narrator: The delegates to the Constitutional Convention were deeply divided over who should lead the new government they were creating. Some delegates, like Alexander Hamilton, wanted a president to serve for many years or even a lifetime, like a king. Others wanted the office to have little real power and the term to be only one or two years.

Randolph: What we need to create, gentlemen, is a strong national government with a Congress to make laws, a president to enforce those laws, and a judicial branch to determine that they are fair and equitable. Our poor nation right now is a collection of weak and arguing states who don't trust each other. They impose taxes on each other and sometimes are even at the point of war.

Dickinson: We just got rid of one king. I'll not have another one. Keep the states as they are.

Gerry: We were sent here to revise the Articles of Confederation—not to form a nation with a king or some other powerful leader.

Hamilton: This country needs strong leadership—otherwise, it is going to be gobbled up by European empires. What we need is a president for life.

Dickinson: No, I don't agree. A president with very little power is what we desire. The weaker he is, the safer we will be. One year is long enough for any president.

Madison: He has to be strong, or this nation will blow away like leaves in the wind, with every state going broke, being swallowed up by other countries or always getting into wars.

Constitutional Convention *(cont.)*

Gerry: I don't trust any ruler. All he'll want to do is raise taxes and get us into war. He will end up a king with a different title.

Madison: This country needs leadership. We cannot afford to have a weak or feeble chief executive. He must be able to act with force when necessary.

Narrator: Many delegates were fearful that the presidency would pass from father to son like a monarchy, or that the president would rule the country without regard to the Congress or the rule of law.

Gerry: Why does it have to be a president for life? Why not for six years or four or one year?

Hamilton: Well, it would be embarrassing to have a lot of ex-presidents wandering around like ghosts with nothing much to do.

Franklin: But suppose you had a lifetime president, or even one with a six-year term, and he turned out to be a worthless president. What could you do about it? We might have to arrange some way to get rid of a president who is incompetent or sick or who commits a crime. Otherwise, we might have to shoot him.

Narrator: Many of the delegates were amused by Ben Franklin's suggestion, but they also recognized the problem. What would ex-presidents do? Would they go back home to their businesses and farms, or would they find other jobs in government? The delegates were also uncertain about what to call the leader of this new office they were creating.

Gerry: How will we address this president?

Hamilton: I think that he should be called His Highness or His Excellency.

Gerry: Sounds just like a king to me or some other high-fallutin' gentry.

Franklin: How about just plain "Mister," such as "Mr. Randolph" or "Mr. Madison"?

Gerry: How about "Mr. President"? It's simple, dignified, and it doesn't put on airs.

Dickinson: That sounds just right.

Readers' Theater

Before You Read

"Meet Paul Bunyan" is an example of a tall tale. The authors of tall tales are usually unknown, because the tales have been told and retold for hundreds of years. The details in tall tales often change and became even more incredible as time goes on.

Meet Paul Bunyan

Characters

- Narrator 1
- Narrator 2
- Paul Bunyan
- Babe, the Blue Ox

Narrator 1: In a time too long ago for even history books, America was one large forest. Thick, dark forests grew all across the country then from sea to shining sea.

Narrator 2: And Paul Bunyan was the greatest lumberjack there ever was. He was a mighty giant of a man.

Paul Bunyan: My name is Paul Bunyan. I'm the greatest lumberjack there ever was! I am a mighty giant of a man.

Narrator 1: Paul was so big that it took five giant storks to carry that huge bundle of joy to his parents.

Narrator 2: Paul Bunyan was so big that he could eat 40 barrels of baby cereal.

Narrator 1: Paul was so big that he used tree tops to comb out his wiry black beard.

Narrator 2: Paul was so big that, on cold days, his breath made steam clouds that blocked the sun all day long.

Narrator 1: Everywhere Paul went in the wild north woods, Babe, his blue ox, went with him.

Paul Bunyan: Yessiree! This is my trusted friend, Babe.

Babe: That's me! I am Babe, the blue ox. I am the greatest, bluest beast there ever was.

Meet Paul Bunyan *(cont.)*

Narrator 1:   Babe measured 42 ax handles high. (By the way, an ax-handle is about a foot and a half long.)

Narrator 2:   It took a crow one whole day to fly between Babe's horns. And when Babe bellowed, it shook the trees down to their roots.

Babe: Some folks think they hear thunder. But, no! It was just my bellowing.

Narrator 1:   Paul rescued Babe as a calf. Paul saved him from freezing during the winter of Blue Snow.

Paul Bunyan: Babe is so strong that he can pull anything that has two ends.

Babe: Except Paul! And Paul will never let me push him!

Narrator 2:   Paul once used Babe to straighten out 30 miles of crooked town road!

Paul Bunyan: Babe, you are the greatest, bluest beast that ever was. Now, you take the end of this crooked road and pull. Pull, Babe, pull! Pull, Babe, pull!

Narrator 1:   Babe is so strong that he can pull anything that had two ends. Babe pulled and pulled. He pulled and pulled.

Narrator 2:   When Babe had pulled all the twists and curves straight, there were an extra 12 miles of road left over.

Babe: Paul rolled it all up and gave it back to the town to use elsewhere.

Narrator 1:   That proves it: Paul Bunyan is a mighty giant of a man.

Narrator 2:   And Babe is the greatest, bluest beast that ever was!

Before You Read

Some of the authors below wrote about experiences they had as children, while others wrote about fantastical creatures in different worlds. Do you like realistic fiction, fantasy, or another type of writing?

Famous Authors

Characters

- Talk Show Host
- Mark Twain
- Louisa May Alcott
- Roald Dahl
- C.S. Lewis
- J.R.R. Tolkien

Talk Show Host: Today, we are lucky enough to host five famous children's authors on our talk show. Welcome! Can you tell us a little about yourselves?

Twain: I am famous for two of my books in particular: Tom Sawyer and The Adventures of Huckleberry Finn. I worked on the Mississipi River in my youth, and I found inspiration for my books in this experience. I believed that humor was a good way to get important points across in my writing.

Alcott: I'm most famous for my novel Little Women. But I also loved to write mystery novels for adults. I grew up on a farm with my father, Bronson, who was a famous philosopher. We often had little money, but my mother encouraged creativity and made life fun for my sisters and me. I've put many of our experiences into my novels.

Dahl: I loved writing books for children. I wrote James and the Giant Peach and Charlie and the Chocolate Factory. I grew up in Wales and went to an English boarding school. One of my main hobbies was reading.

Lewis: My full name was Clive Staples Lewis. I was born in Ireland, and fought for the British army in World War I. I began publishing The Chronicles of Narnia when I was 52. I also wrote books for adults.

Tolkien: My full name was John Ronald Tolkien. I was born in South Africa and then moved to England. My family didn't have much money, but I received a good education. I could speak several languages, and I even made up some of my own! I became a professor at Oxford and began writing a story about a creature I called a "hobbit."

Narrator: You all sound absolutely fascinating. Do you have any advice for young writers out there in the audience?

Twain: Keep a sense of humor.

Alcott: Write every day.

Dahl: Read every day.

Lewis: Cultivate your imagination.

Tolkien: Study hard, and take risks in your writing.

Narrator: Thank you very much for your excellent advice!